Snap Dragons: A Tale Of Christmas Eve And Old Father Christmas, An Old Fashioned Tale Of The Young Days Of A Grumpy Old Godfather

Juliana Horatia Gatty Ewing

In the interest of creating a more extensive selection of rare historical book reprints, we have chosen to reproduce this title even though it may possibly have occasional imperfections such as missing and blurred pages, missing text, poor pictures, markings, dark backgrounds and other reproduction issues beyond our control. Because this work is culturally important, we have made it available as a part of our commitment to protecting, preserving and promoting the world's literature. Thank you for your understanding.

SNAP-DRAGONS

A Tale of Christmas Eve

AND

Old Father Christmas

An Old-Fashioned Tale of the Young Days of a Grumpy Old Godfather.

BY

JULIANA HORATIA EWING

AUTHOR OF "JACKANAPES" ETC., ETC.

ILLUSTRATED BY GORDON BROWNE.

ENGRAVED AND PRINTED BY EDMUND EVANS.

LONDON
SOCIETY FOR PROMOTING CHRISTIAN KNOWLEDGE,
NORTHUMBERLAND AVENUE, CHARING CROSS, W.C.
43, QUEEN VICTORIA STREET, E.C.;
26, ST. GEORGE'S PLACE, HYDE PARK CORNER, S.W.
BRIGHTON: 135, NORTH STREET.
NEW YORK: E. & J. B. YOUNG & CO.

"With one breath we exclaimed, '*It's Old Father Christmas!*'"

PAGE 57.

SNAP-DRAGONS

A Tale of Christmas Eve.

MR. AND MRS SKRATDJ.

ONCE upon a time there lived a certain family of the name of Skratdj. (It has a Russian or Polish look, and yet they most certainly lived in England.) They were remarkable for the following peculiarity. They seldom seriously quarrelled, but they never agreed about anything. It is hard to say whether it were more painful for their friends to hear them constantly contradicting each other, or gratifying to discover that it "meant nothing," and was "only their way."

It began with the father and mother. They were a worthy couple, and really attached to each other. But they had a habit of contradicting each other's statements, and opposing each other's opinions, which, though mutually understood and allowed for in private, was most trying to the by-standers in public. If one related an anecdote, the other would break in with half-a-dozen corrections of trivial details of no interest or importance to anyone, the speakers included. For instance: Suppose the two dining in a strange house, and Mrs. Skratdj seated by the host, and contributing to the small-talk of the dinner-table. Thus:—

"Oh yes. Very changeable weather indeed. It looked quite promising yesterday morning in the town, but it began to rain at noon."

"A quarter past eleven, my dear," Mr. Skratdj's voice would be heard to say from several chairs down, in the corrective tones of a husband and a father; "and really, my dear, so far from being a promising morning, I must say it looked about as threatening as it well could. Your memory is not always accurate in small matters, my love."

But Mrs. Skratdj had not been a wife and a mother for fifteen years, to be snuffed out at one snap of the marital snuffers. As Mr. Skratdj leaned forward in his chair, she leaned forward in hers, and defended herself across the intervening couples.

"Why, my dear Mr. Skratdj, you said yourself the weather had not been so promising for a week."

"What I said, my dear, pardon me, was that the barometer was higher than it had been for a week. But, as you might have observed if these details were in your line, my love, which they are not, the rise was extraordinarily rapid, and there is no surer sign of unsettled weather.—But Mrs. Skratdj is apt to forget these unimportant trifles," he added, with a comprehensive smile round the dinner-table; "her thoughts are very properly absorbed by the more important domestic questions of the nursery."

"Now I think that's rather unfair on Mr. Skratdj's part," Mrs. Skratdj would chirp, with a smile quite as affable and as general as her husband's. "I'm sure he's *quite* as forgetful and inaccurate as *I* am. And I don't think *my* memory is at *all* a bad one."

"You forgot the dinner hour when we were going out to dine last week, nevertheless," said Mr. Skratdj.

"And you couldn't help me when I asked you," was the sprightly retort. "And I'm sure it's not like you to forget anything about *dinner*, my dear."

"The letter was addressed to you," said Mr. Skratdj.

"I sent it to you by Jemima," said Mrs. Skratdj.

"I didn't read it," said Mr. Skratdj.

"Well, you burnt it," said Mrs. Skratdj; "and, as I always say, there's nothing more foolish than burning a letter of invitation before the day, for one is certain to forget."

"I've no doubt you always do say it," Mr. Skratdj remarked, with a smile, "but I certainly never remember to have heard the observation from your lips, my love."

"Whose memory's in fault there?" asked Mrs. Skratdj triumphantly; and as at this point the ladies rose, Mrs. Skratdj had the last word.

Indeed, as may be gathered from this conversation, Mrs. Skratdj was quite able to defend herself. When she was yet a bride, and young and timid, she used to collapse when Mr. Skratdj contradicted her statements, and set her stories straight in public. Then she hardly ever opened her lips without disappearing under the domestic extinguisher. But in the course of fifteen years she had learned that Mr. Skratdj's bark was a great deal worse than his bite. (If, indeed, he had a bite at all.) Thus snubs that made other people's ears tingle, had no effect whatever on the lady to whom they were addressed, for she knew exactly what they were worth, and had by this time become fairly adept at snapping in return. In the days when she succumbed she was occasionally unhappy, but now she and her husband understood each other, and having agreed to differ, they unfortunately agreed also to differ in public.

Indeed, it was the by-standers who had the worst of it on these occasions. To the worthy couple themselves the habit had become second nature, and in no way affected the friendly tenour of their domestic relations. They would interfere with each other's conversation, contradicting assertions, and disputing conclusions for a whole evening; and then, when all the world and his wife thought that these ceaseless sparks of bickering must blaze up into a flaming quarrel as soon as they were alone, they would bowl amicably home in a cab, criticizing the friends who were commenting upon them, and as little agreed about the events of the evening as about the details of any other events whatever.

Yes. The by-standers certainly had the worst of it. Those who were near wished themselves anywhere else, especially when appealed to. Those who were at a distance did not mind so much. A domestic squabble at a certain distance is interesting, like an engagement viewed from a point beyond the range of guns. In such a position one may some day be placed oneself! Moreover, it gives a touch of excitement to a dull evening to be able to say *sotto voce* to one's neighbour, "Do listen! The Skratdjs are at it again!" Their unmarried friends thought a terrible abyss of tyranny and aggravation must lie beneath it all, and blessed their stars that they were still single, and able to tell a tale their own way. The married ones had more idea of how it really was, and wished in the name of common sense and good taste that Skratdj and his wife would not make fools of themselves.

So it went on, however; and so, I suppose, it goes on still, for not many bad habits are cured in middle age.

On certain questions of comparative speaking their views were never identical. Such as the temperature being hot or cold, things being light or dark, the apple-tarts being sweet or sour. So one day Mr Skratdj came into the room, rubbing his hands, and planting himself at the fire with "Bitterly cold it is to-day, to be sure."

"Why, my dear William," said Mrs. Skratdj, "I'm

sure you must have got a cold; I feel a fire quite oppressive myself."

"You were wishing you'd a seal-skin jacket yesterday, when it wasn't half as cold as it is to-day," said Mr. Skratdj.

"My dear William! Why, the children were shivering the whole day, and the wind was in the north."

"Due east, Mrs. Skratdj."

"I know by the smoke," said Mrs. Skratdj, softly but decidedly.

"I fancy I can tell an east wind when I feel it," said Mr. Skratdj, jocosely, to the company.

"I told Jemima to look at the weathercock," murmured Mrs. Skratdj.

"I don't care a fig for Jemima," said her husband.

On another occasion Mrs. Skratdj and a lady friend were conversing.

. . . "We met him at the Smiths'—a gentlemanlike agreeable man, about forty," said Mrs. Skratdj, in reference to some matter interesting to both ladies.

"Not a day over thirty-five," said Mr. Skratdj, from behind his newspaper.

"Why, my dear William, his hair's grey," said Mrs. Skratdj.

"Plenty of men are grey at thirty," said Mr. Skratdj. "I knew a man who was grey at twenty-five."

"Well, forty or thirty-five, it doesn't much matter," said Mrs. Skratdj, about to resume her narration.

"Five years matter a good deal to most people at thirty-five," said Mr. Skratdj, as he walked towards the door. "They would make a remarkable difference to me, I know;" and with a jocular air Mr. Skratdj departed, and Mrs. Skratdj had the rest of the anecdote her own way.

THE LITTLE SKRATDJS.

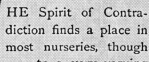

THE Spirit of Contradiction finds a place in most nurseries, though to a very varying degree in different ones. Children snap and snarl by nature, like young puppies; and most of us can remember taking part in some such spirited dialogues as the following:—

{ "I will."
{ "You can't."

{ "You shall."
{ "I won't."

{ "You daren't."
{ "I dare."

{ "I'll tell Mamma."
{ "I don't care if you do."

It is the part of wise parents to repress these squibs and crackers of juvenile contention, and to enforce that slowly-learned lesson, that in this world one must often "pass over" and "put up with" things in other people, being oneself by no means perfect. Also that it is a kindness, and almost a duty, to let people think and say and do things in their own way occasionally.

But even if Mr. and Mrs. Skratdj had ever thought of teaching all this to their children, it must be confessed that the lesson would not have come with a good grace from either of them, since they snapped and snarled between themselves as much or more than their children in the nursery.

The two eldest were the leaders in the nursery squabbles. Between these, a boy and a girl, a ceaseless war of words was waged from morning to night. And as neither of them lacked ready wit, and both were in constant practice, the art of snapping was cultivated by them to the highest pitch.

It began at breakfast, if not sooner.

"You've taken my chair."

"It's not your chair."

"You know it's the one I like, and it was in my place."

"How do you know it was in your place?"

"Never mind. I do know."

"No, you don't."

"Yes, I do."

"Suppose I say it was in my place."

"You can't, for it wasn't."

"I can, if I like."

"Well, was it?"

"I sha'n't tell you."

"Ah! that shews it wasn't."

"No, it doesn't."

"Yes, it does."

Etc., etc., etc.

The direction of their daily walks was a fruitful subject of difference of opinion.

"Let's go on the Common to-day, Nurse."

"Oh, don't let's go there; we're always going on the Common."

"I'm sure we're not. We've not been there for ever so long."

"Oh, what a story! We were there on Wednesday. Let's go down Gipsey Lane. We never go down Gipsey Lane."

"Why, we're always going down Gipsey Lane. And there's nothing to see there."

"I don't care. I won't go on the Common, and I shall go and get Papa to say we're to go down Gipsey Lane. I can run faster than you."

"That's very sneaking; but I don't care."

"Papa! Papa! Polly's called me a sneak."

"No, I didn't, Papa."

"You did."

"No, I didn't. I only said it was sneaking of you to say you'd run faster than me, and get Papa to say we were to go down Gipsey Lane."

"Then you did call him sneaking," said Mr. Skratdj. "And you're a very naughty ill-mannered little girl. You're getting very troublesome, Polly, and I shall have to send you to school, where you'll be kept in order. Go where your brother wishes at once."

For Polly and her brother had reached an age when it was convenient, if possible, to throw the blame of all nursery differences on Polly. In families where domestic discipline is rather fractious than firm, there comes a stage when the girls almost invariably go to the wall, because they will stand snubbing, and the boys will not. Domestic authority, like some other powers, is apt to be magnified on the weaker class.

But Mr. Skratdj would not always listen even to Harry.

"If you don't give it me back directly, I'll tell about your eating the two magnum-bonums in the kitchen garden on Sunday," said Master Harry on one occasion.

> " Tell-tale tit!
> Your tongue shall be slit,
> And every dog in the town shall have a little bit,"

quoted his sister.

"Ah! You've called me a tell-tale. Now I'll go and tell Papa. You got into a fine scrape for calling me names the other day."

"Go, then! I don't care."

"You wouldn't like me to go, I know."

"You daren't. That's what it is."

"I dare."

"Then why don't you?"

"Oh, I am going; but you'll see what will be the end of it."

Polly, however, had her own reasons for remaining stolid, and Harry started. But when he reached the landing he paused. Mr. Skratdj had especially announced that morning that he did not wish to be disturbed, and though he was a favourite, Harry had no desire to invade the dining-room at this crisis. So he returned to the nursery, and said with a magnanimous air, "I don't want to get you into a scrape, Polly. If you'll beg my pardon I won't go."

"I'm sure I sha'n't," said Polly, who was equally well informed as to the position of affairs at head-quarters. "Go, if you dare."

"I won't if you want me not," said Harry, discreetly waiving the question of apologies.

"But I'd rather you went," said the obdurate Polly. "You're always telling tales. Go and tell now, if you're not afraid."

So Harry went. But at the bottom of the stairs he lingered again, and was meditating how to return with most credit to his dignity, when Polly's face appeared through the banisters, and Polly's sharp tongue goaded him on.

"Ah! I see you. You're stopping. You daren't go."

"I dare," said Harry; and at last he went.

As he turned the handle of the door, Mr. Skratdj turned round.

"Please, Papa——" Harry began.

"Get away with you!" cried Mr. Skratdj. "Didn't

I tell you I was not to be disturbed this morning? What an extraor——"

But Harry had shut the door, and withdrawn precipitately.

Once outside, he returned to the nursery with dignified steps, and an air of apparent satisfaction, saying,

"You're to give me the bricks, please."

"Who says so?"

"Why, who should say so? Where have I been, pray?"

"I don't know, and I don't care."

"I've been to Papa. There!"

"Did he say I was to give up the bricks?"

"I've told you."

"No, you've not."

"I sha'n't tell you any more."

"Then I'll go to Papa and ask."

"Go by all means."

"I won't if you'll tell me truly."

"I sha'n't tell you anything. Go and ask, if you dare," said Harry, only too glad to have the tables turned.

Polly's expedition met with the same fate, and she attempted to cover her retreat in a similar manner.

"Ah! you didn't tell."

"I don't believe you asked Papa."

"Don't you? Very well!"

"Well, did you?"

"Never mind."

Etc., etc., etc.

Meanwhile Mr. Skratdj scolded Mrs. Skratdj for not keeping the children in better order. And Mrs. Skratdj said it was quite impossible to do so, when Mr. Skratdj spoilt Harry as he did, and weakened her (Mrs. Skratdj's) authority by constant interference.

Difference of sex gave point to many of these nursery squabbles, as it so often does to domestic broils.

"Boys never will do what they're asked," Polly would complain.

"Girls ask such unreasonable things," was Harry's retort.

"Not half so unreasonable as the things you ask."

"Ah! that's a different thing! Women have got to do what men tell them, whether it's reasonable or not."

"No, they've not!" said Polly. "At least, that's only husbands and wives."

"All women are inferior animals," said Harry.

"Try ordering Mamma to do what you want, and see!" said Polly.

"Men have got to give orders, and women have to obey," said Harry, falling back on the general principle. "And when I get a wife, I'll take care I make her do what I tell her. But you'll have to obey your husband when you get one."

"I won't have a husband, and then I can do as I like."

"Oh, won't you? You'll try to get one, I know. Girls always want to be married."

"I'm sure I don't know why," said Polly; "they must have had enough of men if they have brothers."

And so they went on, *ad infinitum*, with ceaseless arguments that proved nothing and convinced nobody, and a continual stream of contradiction that just fell short of downright quarrelling.

Indeed, there was a kind of snapping even less near to a dispute than in the cases just mentioned. The little Skratdjs, like some other children, were under the unfortunate delusion that it sounds clever to hear little boys and girls snap each other up with smart sayings, and old and rather vulgar play upon words, such as:

"I'll give you a Christmas box. Which ear will you have it on?"

"I won't stand it."

"Pray take a chair."

"You shall have it to-morrow."

"To-morrow never comes."

And so if a visitor kindly began to talk to one of the children, another was sure to draw near and "take up" all the first child's answers, with smart comments, and catches that sounded as silly as they were tiresome and impertinent.

And ill-mannered as this was, Mr. and Mrs. Skratdj never put a stop to it. Indeed, it was only a caricature of what they did themselves. But they often said, "We can't think how it is the children are always squabbling!"

THE SKRATDJ'S DOG AND THE HOT-TEMPERED GENTLEMAN.

IT is wonderful how the state of mind of a whole household is influenced by the heads of it. Mr. Skratdj was a very kind master, and Mrs. Skratdj was a very kind mistress, and yet their servants lived in a perpetual fever of irritability that just fell short of discontent. They jostled each other on the back stairs, said sharp things in the pantry, and kept up a perennial warfare on the subject of the duty of the sexes with the general manservant. They gave warning on the slightest provocation.

The very dog was infected by the snapping mania. He was not a brave dog, he was not a vicious dog, and no high-breeding sanctioned his pretensions to arrogance. But like his owners, he had contracted a bad habit, a trick, which made him the pest of all timid visitors, and indeed of all visitors whatsoever.

The moment anyone approached the house, on certain occasions when he was spoken to, and often in no traceable connection with any cause at all, Snap the mongrel would rush out, and bark in his little sharp voice—"Yap! yap! yap!" If the visitor made a stand, he would bound away sideways on his four little legs; but the moment the visitor went on his way again, Snap was at his heels—"Yap! yap! yap!" He barked at the milkman, the butcher's boy, and the baker, though he saw them every day. He never got used to the washer-woman, and she never got used to him. She said he "put her in mind of that there black dog in the Pilgrim's Progress." He sat at the gate in summer, and yapped at every vehicle and every pedestrian who ventured to pass on the high road. He never but once had the

chance of barking at burglars; and then, though he barked long and loud, nobody got up, for they said, "It's only Snap's way." The Skratdjs lost a silver tea-pot, a Stilton cheese, and two electro christening mugs, on this occasion; and Mr. and Mrs. Skratdj dispute who it was who discouraged reliance on Snap's warning to the present day.

THE SANDY GENTLEMAN'S WAY.

One Christmas time, a certain hot-tempered gentleman came to visit the Skratdjs. A tall, sandy, energetic young man, who carried his own bag from the railway. The bag had been crammed rather than packed, after the wont of bachelors; and you could see where the heel of a boot distended the leather, and where the bottle of shaving-cream lay.

As he came up to the house, out came Snap as usual—"Yap! yap! yap!" Now the gentleman was very fond of dogs, and had borne this greeting some dozen of times from Snap, who for his part knew the visitor quite as well as the washerwoman, and rather better than the butcher's boy. The gentleman had good, sensible, well-behaved dogs of his own, and was greatly disgusted with Snap's conduct. Nevertheless he spoke friendly to him; and Snap, who had had many a bit from his plate, could not help stopping for a minute to lick his hand. But no sooner did the gentleman proceed on his way, than Snap flew at his heels in the usual fashion—

"Yap! Yap! Yap!"

On which the gentleman—being hot-tempered, and one of those people with whom it is (as they say) a word and a blow, and the blow first—made a dash at Snap, and Snap taking to his heels, the gentleman flung his carpet-bag after him. The bottle of shaving-cream hit upon a stone and was smashed. The heel of the boot caught Snap on the back, and sent him squealing to the kitchen. And he never barked at that gentleman again.

SNAPPING TURTLES.

If the gentleman disapproved of Snap's conduct, he still less liked the continual snapping of the Skratdj family themselves. He was an old friend of Mr. and Mrs. Skratdj, however, and knew that they were really happy together, and that it was only a bad habit which made them constantly contradict each other. It was in allusion to their real affection for each other, and their perpetual disputing, that he called them the "Snapping Turtles."

When the war of words waxed hottest at the dinner-table between his host and hostess, he would drive his hands through his shock of sandy hair, and say, with a comical glance out of his umber eyes, "Don't flirt, my friends. It makes a bachelor feel awkward."

And neither Mr. nor Mrs. Skratdj could help laughing.

With the little Skratdjs his measures were more vigorous. He was very fond of children, and a good friend to them. He grudged no time or trouble to help them in their games and projects, but he would not tolerate their snapping up each other's words in his presence. He was much more truly kind than many visitors, who think it polite to smile at the sauciness and forwardness which ignorant vanity leads children so often to "shew off" before strangers. These civil acquaintances only abuse both children and parents behind their backs, for the very bad habits which they help to encourage.

The hot-tempered gentleman's treatment of his young friends was very different. One day he was talking to Polly, and making some kind inquiries about her lessons, to which she was replying in a quiet and sensible fashion, when up came Master Harry, and began to display his wit by comments on the conversation, and by snapping at and contradicting his sister's remarks, to which she retorted; and the usual snap-dialogue went on as usual.

"Then you like music," said the hot-tempered gentleman.

"Yes, I like it very much," said Polly.

"Oh, do you?" Harry broke in. "Then what are you always crying over it for?"

"I'm not always crying over it.

"Yes, you are."

"No, I'm not. I only cry sometimes, when I stick fast."

"Your music must be very sticky, for you're always stuck fast."

"Hold your tongue!" said the hot-tempered gentleman.

With what he imagined to be a very waggish air, Harry put out his tongue, and held it with his finger and thumb. It was unfortunate that he had not time to draw it in again before the hot-tempered gentleman gave him a stinging box on the ear, which brought his teeth rather sharply together on the tip of his tongue, which was bitten in consequence.

"It's no use *speaking*," said the hot-tempered gentleman, driving his hands through his hair.

Children are like dogs, they are very good judges of their real friends. Harry did not like the hot-tempered gentleman a bit the less because he was obliged to respect and obey him; and all the children welcomed him boisterously when he arrived that Christmas which we have spoken of in connection with his attack on Snap.

It was on the morning of Christmas Eve that the china punch bowl was broken. Mr. Skratdj had a warm dispute with Mrs. Skratdj as to whether it had been kept in a safe place; after which both had a brisk encounter with the housemaid, who did not know how it happened; and she, flouncing down the back passage, kicked Snap; who forthwith flew at the gardener as he was bringing in the horse-radish for the beef; who stepping backwards trode upon the cat; who spit and swore, and went up the pump with her tail as big as a fox's brush.

To avoid this domestic scene, the hot-tempered gentleman withdrew to the breakfast-room and took up a newspaper. By-and-by, Harry and Polly came in, and they were soon snapping comfortably over their own affairs in a corner.

The hot-tempered gentleman's umber eyes had been looking over the top of his newspaper at them for some time, before he called, "Harry, my boy!"

And Harry came up to him.

"Shew me your tongue, Harry," said he.

"What for?" said Harry; "you're not a doctor."

"Do as I tell you," said the hot-tempered gentleman; and as Harry saw his hand moving, he put his tongue out with all possible haste. The hot-tempered gentleman sighed. "Ah!" he said in depressed tones; "I thought so!—Polly, come and let me look at yours."

Polly, who had crept up during this process, now put

out hers. But the hot-tempered gentleman looked gloomier still, and shook his head.

"What is it?" cried both the children. "What do you mean?" And they seized the tips of their tongues in their fingers, to feel for themselves.

But the hot-tempered gentleman went slowly out of the room without answering; passing his hands through his hair, and saying, "Ah! Hum!" and nodding with an air of grave foreboding.

Just as he crossed the threshold, he turned back, and put his head into the room. "Have you ever noticed that your tongues are growing pointed?" he asked.

"No!" cried the children with alarm. "Are they?"

"If ever you find them becoming forked," said the gentleman in solemn tones, "let me know."

With which he departed, gravely shaking his head.

In the afternoon the children attacked him again.

"*Do* tell us what's the matter with our tongues."

"You were snapping and squabbling just as usual this morning," said the hot-tempered gentleman.

"Well, we forgot," said Polly. "We don't mean anything, you know. But never mind that now, please. Tell us about our tongues. What is going to happen to them?"

"I'm very much afraid," said the hot-tempered gentleman, in solemn measured tones, "that you are both of you—fast—going—to—the—"

"Dogs?" suggested Harry, who was learned in cant expressions.

"Dogs!" said the hot-tempered gentleman, driving his hands through his hair. "Bless your life, no! Nothing half so pleasant! (That is, unless all dogs were like Snap, which mercifully they are not.) No, my sad fear is, that you are both of you—rapidly—going—*to the Snap-Dragons!*"

And not another word would the hot-tempered gentleman say on the subject.

Christmas Eve.

In the course of a few hours Mr. and Mrs. Skratdj recovered their equanimity. The punch was brewed in a jug, and tasted quite as good as usual. The evening was very lively. There were a Christmas tree, Yule cakes, log, and candles, furmety, and snap-dragon after supper. When the company was tired of the tree, and had gained an appetite by the hard exercise of stretching to high branches, blowing out "dangerous" tapers, and cutting ribbon and pack-thread in all directions, supper came, with its welcome cakes and furmety and punch. And when furmety somewhat palled upon the taste (and it must be admitted to boast more sentiment than flavour as a Christmas dish), the Yule candles were blown out and both the spirits and the palates of the party were stimulated by the mysterious and pungent pleasures of snap-dragon.

Then, as the hot-tempered gentleman warmed his coat-tails at the Yule-log, a grim smile stole over his features as he listened to the sounds in the room. In the darkness the blue flames leaped and danced, the

THE FAMILY CIRCLE, AND FAMILY JARS.   31

raisins were snapped and snatched from hand to hand, scattering fragments of flame hither and thither. The children shouted as the fiery sweetmeats burnt away the mawkish taste of the furmety. Mr. Skratdj cried that they were spoiling the carpet; Mrs. Skratdj complained that he had spilled some brandy on her dress. Mr. Skratdj retorted that she should not wear dresses so

susceptible of damage in the family circle. Mrs. Skratdj recalled an old speech of Mr. Skratdj on the subject of wearing one's nice things for the benefit of one's family, and not reserving them for visitors. Mr. Skratdj remembered that Mrs. Skratdj's excuse for buying that particular dress when she did not need it, was her intention of keeping it for the next year. The children disputed as to the credit for courage and the amount of raisins due to each. Snap barked furiously at the flames; and the maids hustled each other for good places in the doorway, and would not have allowed the man-servant to see at all, but he looked over their heads.

"St! St! At it! At it!" chuckled the hot-tempered gentleman in undertones. And when he said this, it seemed as if the voices of Mr. and Mrs. Skratdj rose higher in matrimonial repartee, and the children's squabbles became louder, and the dog yelped as if he were mad, and the maids' contest was sharper; whilst the snap-dragon flames leaped up and up, and blue fire flew about the room like foam.

At last the raisins were finished, the flames were all but out, and the company withdrew to the drawing-room. Only Harry lingered.

"Come along, Harry," said the hot-tempered gentleman.

"Wait a minute," said Harry.

"You had better come," said the gentleman.

"Why?" said Harry.

"There's nothing to stop for. The raisins are eaten, the brandy is burnt out——"

"No, it's not," said Harry.

"Well, almost. It would be better if it were quite out. Now come. It's dangerous for a boy like you to be alone with the Snap-Dragons to-night."

"Fiddle-sticks!" said Harry.

"Go your own way, then!" said the hot-tempered gentleman; and he bounced out of the room, and Harry was left alone.

Dancing with the Dragons.

HE crept up to the table, where one little pale blue flame flickered in the snap-dragon dish.

"What a pity it should go out!" said Harry. At this moment the brandy bottle on the side-board caught his eye.

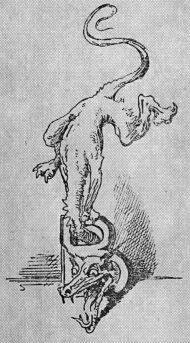

"Just a little more," murmured Harry to himself; and he uncorked the bottle, and poured a little brandy on to the flame.

Now of course, as soon as the brandy touched the fire, all the brandy in the bottle blazed up at once, and the bottle split to pieces; and it was very fortunate for Harry that he did not get seriously hurt. A little of the hot brandy did get into his eyes, and made them smart, so that he had to shut them for a few seconds.

UT when he opened them again, what a sight he saw! All over the room the blue flames leaped and danced as they had leaped and danced in the soup-plate with the raisins. And Harry saw that each successive flame was the fold in the long body of a bright blue Dragon, which moved like the body of a snake. And the room was full of these Dragons. In the face they were like the dragons one sees made of very old blue and white china; and they had forked tongues, like the tongues of serpents. They were most beautiful in colour, being sky-blue. Lobsters who have just changed their coats are very handsome, but the violet and indigo of a lobster's coat is nothing to the brilliant sky-blue of a Snap-Dragon.

How they leaped about! They were for ever leaping over each other, like seals at play. But if it was "play" at all with them, it was of a very rough kind; for as they jumped, they snapped and barked at each other, and their barking was like that of the barking Gnu in the Zoological Gardens; and from time to time they tore the hair out of each other's heads with their claws, and scattered it about the floor. And as it dropped it was like the flecks of flame people shake from their fingers when they are eating snap-dragon raisins.

Harry stood aghast.

"What fun!" said a voice close by him; and he saw that one of the Dragons was lying near, and not joining in the game. He had lost one of the forks of his tongue by accident, and could not bark for awhile.

"I'm glad you think it funny," said Harry, "I don't."

"That's right. Snap away!" sneered the Dragon. "You're a perfect treasure. They'll take you in with them the third round."

"Not those creatures?" cried Harry.

"Yes, those creatures. And if I hadn't lost my bark, I'd be the first to lead you off," said the Dragon. "Oh, the game will exactly suit you."

"What is it, please?" Harry asked.

"You'd better not say 'please' to the others," said the Dragon, "if you don't want to have all your hair pulled out. The game is this. You have always to be jumping over somebody else, and you must either talk or bark. If anybody speaks to you, you must snap in return. I need not explain what *snapping* is. *You know.* If anyone by accident gives a civil answer, a claw-full of hair is torn out of his head to stimulate his brain. Nothing can be funnier."

"I dare say it suits you capitally," said Harry; "but I'm sure we shouldn't like it. I mean men and women and children. It wouldn't do for us at all."

"Wouldn't it?" said the Dragon. "You don't know how many human beings dance with dragons on Christmas Eve. If we are kept going in a house till after midnight, we can pull people out of their beds, and take them to dance in Vesuvius."

"Vesuvius!" cried Harry.

"Yes, Vesuvius. We come from Italy originally, you know. Our skins are the colour of the Bay of Naples. We live on dried grapes and ardent spirits. We have glorious fun in the mountain sometimes. Oh! what snapping, and scratching, and tearing! Delicious! There are times when the squabbling becomes too great, and Mother Mountain won't stand it, and spits us all out, and throws cinders after us. But this is only at times.

GOOD WITS WILL STILL BE JANGLING. 37

We had a charming meeting last year. So many human beings, and how they *can* snap! It was a choice party. So very select. We always have plenty of saucy children, and servants. Husbands and wives too, and quite as many of the former as the latter, if not more. But besides these, we had two vestry-men, a country postmaster, who devoted his talents to insulting the public instead of to learning the postal regulations, three cabmen and two "fares," two young shop-girls from a Berlin wool shop in a town where there was no competition, four commercial travellers, six landladies; six Old Bailey lawyers, several widows from almshouses, seven single gentlemen and nine cats, who swore at everything; a dozen sulphur-coloured screaming cockatoos; a lot of street children from a town; a pack of mongrel curs from the colonies, who snapped at the human beings' heels, and five elderly ladies in their Sunday bonnets with Prayer-books, who had been fighting for good seats in church."

"Dear me!" said Harry.

"If you can find nothing sharper to say than 'Dear me,'" said the Dragon, "you will fare badly, I can tell you. Why, I thought you'd a sharp tongue, but it's not forked yet, I see. Here they are, however. Off with you! And if you value your curls— Snap!"

And before Harry could reply, the Snap-Dragons came on on their third round, and as they passed they swept Harry with them.

He shuddered as he looked at his companions. They

were as transparent as shrimps, but of this lovely cerulæan blue. And as they leaped they barked— "Howf! Howf?"—like barking Gnus; and when they leaped Harry had to leap with them. Besides barking, they snapped and wrangled with each other; and in this Harry must join also.

"Pleasant, isn't it?" said one of the blue Dragons.

"Not at all," snapped Harry.

"That's your bad taste," snapped the blue Dragon.

"No, it's not!" snapped Harry.

"Then it's pride and perverseness. You want your hair combing."

"Oh, please don't!" shrieked Harry, forgetting himself. On which the Dragon clawed a handful of hair out of his head, and Harry screamed, and the blue Dragons barked and danced.

"That made your hair curl, didn't it?" asked another Dragon, leaping over Harry.

"That's no business of yours," Harry snapped, as well as he could for crying.

"It's more my pleasure than business," retorted the Dragon.

"Keep it to yourself, then," snapped Harry.

"I mean to share it with you, when I get hold of your hair," snapped the Dragon.

"Wait till you get the chance," Harry snapped, with desperate presence of mind.

"Do you know whom you're talking to?" roared the Dragon; and he opened his mouth from ear to ear, and shot out his forked tongue in Harry's face; and the boy was so frightened that he forgot to snap, and cried piteously,

"Oh, I beg your pardon, please don't!"

On which the blue Dragon clawed another handful of hair out of his head, and all the Dragons barked as before.

How long the dreadful game went on Harry never exactly knew. Well practised as he was in snapping in the nursery, he often failed to think of a retort, and paid for his unreadiness by the loss of his hair. Oh, how foolish and wearisome all this rudeness and snapping now seemed to him! But on he had to go, wondering all the time how near it was to twelve o'clock, and whether the Snap-Dragons would stay till midnight and take him with them to Vesuvius.

At last, to his joy, it became evident that the brandy was coming to an end. The Dragons moved slower, they could not leap so high, and at last one after another they began to go out.

"Oh, if they only all of them get away before twelve!" thought poor Harry.

At last there was only one. He and Harry jumped about and snapped and barked, and Harry was thinking with joy that he was the last, when the clock in the hall gave that whirring sound which some clocks do before they strike, as if it were clearing its throat.

"Oh, *please* go!" screamed Harry in depair.

The blue Dragon leaped up, and took such a clawfull of hair out of the boy's head, that it seemed as if part of the skin went too. But that leap was his last.

He went out at once, vanishing before the first stroke of twelve. And Harry was left on his face on the floor in the darkness.

Conclusion.

WHEN his friends found him there was blood on his forehead. Harry thought it was where the Dragon had clawed him, but they said it was a cut from a fragment of the broken brandy bottle. The Dragons had disappeared as completely as the brandy.

Harry was cured of snapping. He had had quite enough of it for a lifetime, and the catch-contradictions of the household now made him shudder. Polly had not had the benefit of his experiences, and yet she improved also.

In the first place, snapping, like other kinds of quarrelling, requires two parties to it, and Harry would never be a party to snapping any more. And when he gave civil and kind answers to Polly's smart speeches, she felt ashamed of herself, and did not repeat them.

In the second place, she heard about the Snap-Dragons. Harry told all about it to her and to the hot-tempered gentleman.

"Now do you think it's true?" Polly asked the hot-tempered gentleman.

"Hum! Ha!" said he, driving his hands through his hair. "You know I warned you, you were going to the Snap-Dragons."

*   *   *   *   *   *

Harry and Polly snubbed "the little ones" when they snapped, and utterly discountenanced snapping in the nursery. The example and admonitions of elder children are a powerful instrument of nursery discipline, and before long there was not a "sharp tongue" amongst all the little Skratdjs.

But I doubt if the parents ever were cured. I don't know if they heard the story. Besides, bad habits are not easily cured when one is old.

I fear Mr. and Mrs. Skratdj have yet got to dance with the Dragons.

OLD FATHER CHRISTMAS

An Old-Fashioned Tale of the Young Days of a
Grumpy Old Godfather.

OLD FATHER CHRISTMAS

An Old-Fashioned Tale of the Young Days of a
Grumpy Old Godfather.

───◆•◆•◆───

CHAPTER I.

"CAN you fancy, young people," said Godfather Garbel, winking with his prominent eyes, and moving his feet backwards and forwards in his square shoes, so that you could hear the squeak-leather half a room off—"can you fancy my having been a very little boy, and having a godmother? But I had, and she sent me presents on my birthdays too. And young people did not get presents when I was a child as they get them now. *Grumph!* We had not half so many toys as you have, but we kept them twice as long. I think we were fonder of them too, though they were neither so handsome, nor so expensive as these new-fangled affairs you are always breaking about the house. *Grumph!*

"You see, middle-class folk were more saving then.

My mother turned and dyed her dresses, and when she had done with them, the servant was very glad to have them; but, bless me! your mother's maids dress so much finer than their mistress, I do not think they would say

'thank you' for her best Sunday silk. The bustle's the wrong shape. *Grumph!*

"What's that you are laughing at, little miss? It's *pannier*, is it? Well, well, bustle or pannier, call it what you like; but only donkeys wore panniers in my young days, and many's the ride I've had in them.

"Now as I say, my relations and friends thought twice before they pulled out five shillings in a toy shop, but they didn't forget me, all the same.

"On my eighth birthday my mother gave me a bright blue comforter of her own knitting.

"My little sister gave me a ball. My mother had cut out the divisions from various bits in the rag bag, and my sister had done some of the seaming. It was stuffed with bran, and had a cork inside which had broken from old age, and would no longer fit the pickle jar it belonged to. This made the ball bound when we played 'prisoner's base.'

"My father gave me the broken driving-whip that had lost the lash, and an old pair of his gloves, to play coachman with; these I had long wished for, since next to sailing in a ship, in my ideas, came the honour and glory of driving a coach.

"My whole soul, I must tell you, was set upon being a sailor. In those days I had rather put to sea once on Farmer Fodder's duck-pond than ride twice atop of his hay-waggon; and between the smell of hay and the softness of it, and the height you are up above other folk, and the danger of tumbling off if you don't look out—for hay is elastic as well as soft—you don't easily beat a ride on a hay-waggon for pleasure. But as I say, I'd rather put to sea on the duck-pond, though the best craft I could borrow was the pigstye-door, and a pole to punt with, and the village boys jeering when I got aground, which was most of the time—besides the duck-pond never having a wave on it worth the name, punt as you would, and so shallow you could not have got drowned in it to save your life.

"You're laughing now, little master, are you? But let me tell you that drowning's the death for a sailor, whatever you may think. So I've always maintained, and have given every navigable sea in the known world a chance, though here I am after all, laid up in arm-chairs and feather-beds, to wait for bronchitis or some other slow poison. *Grumph!*

"Well, we must all go as we're called, sailors or landsmen, and as I was saying if I was never to sail a ship, I would have liked to drive a coach. A mail coach, serving His Majesty (Her Majesty now GOD bless her!) carrying the Royal Arms, and bound to go, rough weather and fair. Many's the time I've done it (in play you understand) with that whip and those gloves. Dear! dear! The pains I took to teach my sister Patty to be a highwayman, and jump out on me from the drying ground hedge in the dusk with a 'Stand and deliver!' which she couldn't get out of her throat for fright, and wouldn't jump hard enough for fear of hurting me.

"The whip and the gloves gave me joy, I can tell you; but there was more to come.

"Kitty the servant gave me a shell that she had had by her for years. How I had coveted that shell! It had this remarkable property: when you put it to your ear you could hear the roaring of the sea. I had never seen the sea, but Kitty was born in a fisherman's cottage, and many an hour have I sat by the kitchen fire whilst she told me strange stories of the mighty ocean, and ever and anon she would snatch the shell from the mantlepiece and clap it to my ear, crying, 'There child, you couldn't hear it plainer than that. It's the very moral!'

"When Kitty gave me that shell for my very own I felt that life had little more to offer. I held it to every ear in the house, including the cat's; and, seeing Dick the sexton's son go by with an armful of straw to stuff Guy Fawkes, I ran out, and in my anxiety to make him share the treat, and learn what the sea is like, I clapped the shell to his ear so smartly and unexpectedly, that he, thinking me to have struck him, knocked me down then and there with his bundle of straw. When he understood the rights of the case, he begged my pardon handsomely, and gave me two whole treacle sticks and part of a third out of his breeches' pocket, in return for which I forgave him freely, and promised to let him hear the sea roar on every Saturday half-holiday till farther notice.

"And, speaking of Dick and the straw reminds me that my birthday falls on the fifth of November. From this it came about that I always had to bear a good many jokes about being burnt as a Guy Fawkes; but, on the other hand, I was allowed to make a small bonfire of my own, and to have eight potatoes to roast therein, and eight-pennyworth of crackers to let off in the evening. A potatoe and a pennyworth of crackers for every year of my life.

"On this eighth birthday, having got all the above-named gifts, I cried, in the fulness of my heart, 'There never was such a day!' And yet there was more to come, for the evening coach brought me a parcel, and the parcel was my godmother's picture-book.

"My godmother was a gentlewoman of small means; but she was accomplished. She could make very spirited sketches, and knew how to colour them after they were outlined and shaded in Indian ink. She had a pleasant talent for versifying. She was very industrious. I have it from her own lips that she copied the figures in my picture-book from prints in several different houses at which she visited. They were fancy portraits of characters, most of which were familiar to my mind. There were Guy Fawkes, Punch, his then Majesty the King, Bogy, the Man in the Moon, the Clerk of the Weather Office, a Dunce, and Old Father Christmas. Beneath each sketch was a stanza of my godmother's own composing.

"My godmother was very ingenious. She had been mainly guided in her choice of these characters by the prints she happened to meet with, as she did not trust herself to design a figure. But if she could not get exactly what she wanted, she had a clever knack or tracing an outline of the attitude from some engraving, and altering the figure to suit her purpose in the finished sketch. She was the soul of truthfulness, and the notes she added to the index of contents in my picture-book spoke at once for her honesty in avowing obligations, and her ingenuity in availing herself of opportunities.

They ran thus:—

DRAMATIS PERSONÆ.

No. 1.—GUY FAWKES. Outlined from a figure of a warehouseman rolling a sherry cask into Mr. Rudd's wine vaults. I added the hat, cloak, and boots in the finished drawing.

No 2.—PUNCH. I sketched him from the life.

No. 3.—HIS MOST GRACIOUS MAJESTY THE KING. On a quart jug bought in Cheapside.

No. 4.—BOGY, *with bad boys in the bag on his back.* Outlined from Christian bending under his burden, in my mother's old copy of the "Pilgrim's Progress." The face from Giant Despair.

No 5 and No. 6.—THE MAN IN THE MOON, and THE CLERK OF THE WEATHER OFFICE. From a book of caricatures belonging to Dr. James.

No. 7.—A DUNCE. From a steel engraving framed in rosewood that hangs in my Uncle Wilkinson's parlour.

No. 8.—OLD FATHER CHRISTMAS. From a German book at Lady Littleham's.

CHAPTER II.

MY sister Patty was six years old. We loved each other dearly. The picture-book was almost as much hers as mine. We sat so long together on one big footstool by the fire, with our arms round each other, and the book resting on our knees, that Kitty called down blessings on my godmother's head for having sent a volume that kept us both so long out of mischief.

"'If books was allus as useful as that, they'd do for me,' said she; and though this speech did not mean much, it was a great deal for Kitty to say; since, not being herself an educated person, she naturally thought that 'little enough good comes of larning.'

"Patty and I had our favourites amongst the pictures. Bogy, now, was a character one did not care to think about too near bed-time. I was tired of Guy Fawkes, and thought he looked more natural made of straw, as Dick did him. The Dunce was a little too personal; but Old Father Christmas took our hearts by storm; we had never seen anything like him, though now-a-days you may get a plaster figure of him in any toy-shop at Christmas-time, with hair and beard like cotton-wool, and a Christmas-tree in his hand.

"The custom of Christmas-trees came from Germany. I can remember when they were first introduced into England, and what wonderful things we thought them. Now, every village school has its tree, and the scholars openly discuss whether the presents have been 'good,' or 'mean,' as compared with other trees of former years.

"The first one that I ever saw I believed to have come from good Father Christmas himself; but little boys have grown too wise now to be taken in for their own amusement. They are not excited by secret and mysterious preparations in the back drawing-room; they hardly confess to the thrill—which I feel to this day—when the folding-doors are thrown open, and amid the blaze of tapers, Mamma, like a Fate, advances with her scissors to give every one what falls to his lot.

"Well, young people, when I was eight years old I had

not seen a Christmas-tree, and the first picture of one I ever saw was the picture of that held by Old Father Christmas in my godmother's picture-book.

"' What are those things on the tree?' I asked.

"' Candles,' said my father.

"' No, father, not the candles; the other things?'

"' Those are toys, my son.'

"' Are they ever taken off?'

"' Yes, they are taken off, and given to the children who stand round the tree.'

"Patty and I grasped each other by the hand, and with one voice murmured, 'How kind of Old Father Christmas!'

"By-and-by I asked, 'How old is Father Christmas?'

"My father laughed, and said, 'One thousand eight hundred and thirty years, child,' which was then the year of our Lord, and thus one thousand eight hundred and thirty years since the first great Christmas Day.

"' He *looks* very old,' whispered Patty.

"And I, who was, for my age, what Kitty called 'Bible-learned,' said thoughtfully, and with some puzzledness of mind, 'Then he's older than Methuselah.'

"But my father had left the room, and did not hear my difficulty.

"November and December went by, and still the picture-book kept all its charm for Patty and me; and we pondered on and loved Old Father Christmas as children can love and realize a fancy friend. To those who remember the fancies of their childhood I need say no more.

"Christmas week came, Christmas Eve came. My father and mother were mysteriously and unaccountably busy in the parlour (we had only one parlour), and Patty and I were not allowed to go in. We went into the kitchen, but even here was no place of rest for us. Kitty was 'all over the place,' as she phrased it, and cakes, mince-pies, and puddings were with her. As she justly observed, 'There was no place there for children and books to sit with their toes in the fire, when a body wanted to be at the oven all along. The cat was enough for *her* temper,' she added.

"As to puss, who obstinately refused to take a hint which drove her out into the Christmas frost, she returned again and again with soft steps, and a stupidity that was, I think, affected, to the warm hearth, only to fly at intervals, like a football, before Kitty's hasty slipper.

"We had more sense, or less courage. We bowed to Kitty's behests, and went to the back door.

"Patty and I were hardy children, and accustomed to 'run out' in all weathers, without much extra wrapping up. We put Kitty's shawl over our two heads, and went outside. I rather hoped to see something of Dick, for it was holiday time; but no Dick passed. He was busy helping his father to bore holes in the carved seats of the church, which were to hold sprigs of holly for the morrow—that was the idea of church decoration in my young days. You have improved on your elders there, young people, and I am candid enough to allow it. Still, the sprigs of red and green were better than nothing, and, like your lovely wreaths and pious devices, they made one feel as if the old black wood were bursting into life and leaf again for very Christmas joy!

"And, if one only knelt carefully, they did not scratch his nose," added Godfather Garbel, chuckling and rubbing his own, which was large and rather red.

"Well," he continued, "Dick was busy, and not to be seen. We ran across the little yard and looked over the wall at the end to see if we could see anything or anybody. From this point there was a pleasant meadow field sloping prettily away to a little hill about three-quarters of a mile distant; which, catching some fine breezes from the moors beyond, was held to be a place of cure for whooping-cough, or 'kinkcough,' as it was vulgarly called. Up to the top of this Kitty had dragged me, and carried Patty, when we were recovering from the complaint, as I well remember It was the only 'change of air' we could afford, and I dare say it did as well as if we had gone into badly-drained lodgings at the seaside.

"This hill was now covered with snow, and stood off against the grey sky. The white fields looked vast and dreary in the dusk. The only gay things to be seen were the red berries on the holly hedge, in the little lane—which, running by the end of our back-yard, led up to the Hall— and a fat robin redbreast who was staring at me. I was watching the robin, when Patty, who had been peering out of her corner of Kitty's shawl, gave a great jump that dragged the shawl from our heads, and cried,

"'LOOK!'

CHAPTER III.

I LOOKED. An old man was coming along the lane. His hair and beard were as white as cotton-wool. He had a face like the sort of apple that keeps well in winter; his coat was old and brown. There was snow about him in patches, and he carried a small fir-tree.

"The same conviction seized upon us both. With one breath we exclaimed, '*It's Old Father Christmas!*'

"I know now that it was only an old man of the place, with whom we did not happen to be acquainted, and that he was taking a little fir-tree up to the Hall, to be made into a Christmas-tree. He was a very good-humoured old fellow, and rather deaf, for which he made up by smiling and nodding his head a good deal, and saying, 'Aye, aye, *to* be sure!' at likely intervals.

"As he passed us and met our earnest gaze, he smiled and nodded so affably, that I was bold enough to cry, 'Good-evening, Father Christmas!'

"'Same to you!' said he, in a high-pitched voice.

"'Then you *are* Father Christmas,' said Patty.

"'And a Happy New Year,' was Father Christmas's reply, which rather put me out. But he smiled in such a satisfactory manner, that Patty went on, 'You're very old, aren't you?'

"'So I be, miss, so I be,' said Father Christmas, nodding.

"'Father says you're eighteen hundred and thirty years old,' I muttered.

"'Aye, aye, to be sure,' said Father Christmas, 'I'm a long age.'

"A *very* long age, thought I, and I added, 'You're nearly twice as old as Methuselah, you know,' thinking that this might not have struck him.

"'Aye, aye,' said Father Christmas; but he did not seem to think anything of it. After a pause he held up the tree, and cried, 'D'ye know what this is, little miss?'

"'A Christmas-tree,' said Patty.

"And the old man smiled and nodded.

"I leant over the wall, and shouted, 'But there are no candles.'

"'By-and-by,' said Father Christmas, nodding as before. 'When it's dark they'll all be lighted up. That'll be a fine sight!'

"'Toys too, there'll be, won't there?' screamed Patty.

"Father Christmas nodded his head. 'And sweeties,' he added, expressively.

"I could feel Patty trembling, and my own heart beat fast. The thought which agitated us both, was this—'Was Father Christmas bringing the tree to us?' But very anxiety, and some modesty also, kept us from asking outright.

"Only when the old man shouldered his tree, and prepared to move on, I cried in despair, 'Oh, are you going?'

"'I'm coming back by-and-by,' said he.

"'How soon?' cried Patty.

"'About four o'clock,' said the old man, smiling, 'I'm only going up yonder.'

"And, nodding and smiling as he went, he passed away down the lane.

"'Up yonder.' This puzzled us. Father Christmas had pointed, but so indefinitely, that he might have been pointing to the sky, or the fields, or the little wood at the end of the Squire's grounds. I thought the latter, and suggested to Patty that perhaps he had some place underground, like Aladdin's cave, where he got the candles, and all the pretty things for the tree. This idea pleased us both, and we amused ourselves by wondering what Old Father Christmas would choose for us from his stores in that wonderful hole where he dressed his Christmas-trees.

"'I wonder, Patty,' said I, 'why there's no picture of Father Christmas's dog in the book.' For at the old man's heels in the lane there crept a little brown and white spaniel, looking very dirty in the snow.

"'Perhaps it's a new dog that he's got to take care of his cave,' said Patty.

"When we went indoors we examined the picture afresh by the dim light from the passage window, but there was no dog there.

"My father passed us at this moment, and patted my head. 'Father,' said I, 'I don't know, but I do think Old Father Christmas is going to bring us a Christmas-tree to-night.'

"'Who's been telling you that?' said my father. But he passed on before I could explain that we had seen Father Christmas himself, and had had his word for it that he would return at four o'clock, and that the candles on his tree would be lighted as soon as it was dark.

"We hovered on the outskirts of the rooms till four o'clock came. We sat on the stairs and watched the big clock, which I was just learning to read; and Patty made herself giddy with constantly looking up and counting the four strokes, towards which the hour hand slowly moved. We put our noses into the kitchen now and then, to smell the cakes and get warm, and anon we hung about the parlour door, and were most unjustly accused of trying to peep. What did we care what our mother was doing in the parlour?—we who had seen Old Father Christmas himself, and were expecting him back again every moment!

"At last the church clock struck. The sounds boomed heavily through the frost, and Patty thought there were four of them. Then, after due choking and whirring, our own clock struck, and we counted the strokes quite clearly —one! two! three! four! Then we got Kitty's shawl once more, and stole out into the back-yard. We ran to our old place, and peeped, but could see nothing.

"'We'd better get up on to the wall,' I said; and with some difficulty and distress from rubbing her bare knees against the cold stones, and getting the snow up her sleeves, Patty got on the coping of the little wall. I was just struggling after her, when something warm and something cold coming suddenly against the bare calves of my legs, made me shriek with fright. I came down 'with a run,' and bruised my knees, my elbows, and my chin; and the snow that hadn't gone up Patty's sleeves, went down my neck. Then I found that the cold thing was a dog's nose, and the warm thing was his tongue; and Patty cried from her post of observation, 'It's Father Christmas's dog, and he's licking your legs.'

"It really was the dirty little brown and white spaniel; and he persisted in licking me, and jumping on me, and making curious little noises, that must have meant something if one had known his language. I was rather harassed at the moment. My legs were sore, I was a little afraid of the dog, and Patty was very much afraid of sitting on the wall without me.

"'You won't fall,' I said to her. 'Get down, will you?' I said to the dog.

"'Humpty Dumpty fell off a wall,' said Patty.

"'Bow! wow!' said the dog.

"I pulled Patty down, and the dog tried to pull me down; but when my little sister was on her feet, to my relief, he transferred his attentions to her. When he had jumped at her, and licked her several times, he turned round and ran away.

"'He's gone,' said I; 'I'm so glad.'

"But even as I spoke he was back again, crouching at Patty's feet, and glaring at her with eyes the colour of his ears.

"Now Patty was very fond of animals, and when the dog looked at her she looked at the dog, and then she said to me, 'He wants us to go with him.'

"On which (as if he understood our language, though we were ignorant of his) the spaniel sprang away, and went off as hard as he could; and Patty and I went after him, a dim hope crossing my mind—'Perhaps Father Christmas has sent him for us.'

"This idea was rather favoured by the fact that the dog led us up the lane. Only a little way; then he stopped by something lying in the ditch—and once more we cried in the same breath, 'It's Old Father Christmas!'

CHAPTER IV.

RETURNING from the Hall, the old man had slipped upon a bit of ice, and lay stunned in the snow.

"Patty began to cry. 'I think he's dead,' she sobbed.

"'He is so very old, I don't wonder,' I murmured; 'but perhaps he's not. I'll fetch Father.'

"My father and Kitty were soon on the spot. Kitty was as strong as a man; and they carried Father Christmas between them into the kitchen. There he quickly revived.

"I must do Kitty the justice to say that she did not utter a word of complaint at this disturbance of her labours; and that she drew the old man's chair close up to the oven with her own hand. She was so much affected by the behaviour of his dog, that she admitted him even to the hearth; on which puss, being acute enough to see how matters stood, lay down with her back so close to the spaniel's that Kitty could not expel one without kicking both.

"For our parts, we felt sadly anxious about the tree; otherwise we could have wished for no better treat than to sit at Kitty's round table taking tea with Father Christmas. Our usual fare of thick bread and treacle was to-night exchanged for a delicious variety of cakes, which were none the worse to us for being 'tasters and wasters'—that is, little bits of dough, or shortbread, put in to try the state of the oven, and certain cakes that had got broken or burnt in the baking.

"Well, there we sat, helping Old Father Christmas to tea and cake, and wondering in our hearts what could have become of the tree. But you see, young people, when I was a child, parents were stricter than they are now. Even before Kitty died (and she has been dead many a long year) there was a change, and she said that 'children got to think anything became them.' I think we were taught more honest shame about certain things than I often see in little boys and girls now. We were ashamed of boasting, or being greedy, or selfish; we were ashamed of asking for anything that was not offered to us, and of interrupting grown-up people, or talking about ourselves. Why, papas and mammas now-a-days seem quite proud to let their friends see how bold and greedy and talkative their children can be! A lady said to me the other day, 'You wouldn't believe, Mr. Garbel, how forward dear little Harry is for his age. He has his word in everything, and is not a bit shy! and his papa never comes home from town but Harry runs to ask if he's brought him a present. Papa says he'll be the ruin of him!'

"'Madam,' said I, 'even without your word for it, I am quite aware that your child is forward. He is forward and greedy and intrusive, as you justly point out, and I wish you joy of him when those qualities are fully developed. I think his father's fears are well founded.'

"But, bless me! now-a-days, it's 'Come and tell Mr. Smith what a fine boy you are, and how many houses you can build with your bricks,' or, 'The dear child wants everything he sees,' or 'Little pet never lets Mamma alone for a minute; does she, love?' But in my young days it was, 'Self praise is no recommendation' (as Kitty used to tell me), or, 'You're knocking too hard at No. One' (as my father said when we talked about ourselves), or, 'Little boys should be seen but not heard' (as a rule of conduct 'in company'), or, 'Don't ask for what you want, but take what's given you and be thankful.'

"And so you see, young people, Patty and I felt a delicacy in asking Old Father Christmas about the tree. It was not till we had had tea three times round, with tasters and wasters to match, that Patty said very gently, 'It's quite dark now.' And then she heaved a deep sigh.

"Burning anxiety overcame me. I leant towards Father Christmas, and shouted—I had found out that it was needful to shout,—

"'I suppose the candles are on the tree now?'

"'Just about putting of 'em on,' said Father Christmas.

"'And the presents, too?' said Patty.

"'Aye, aye, *to* be sure,' said Father Christmas, and he smiled delightfully.

"I was thinking what farther questions I might venture upon, when he pushed his cup towards Patty, saying, 'Since you are so pressing, miss, I'll take another dish.'

"And Kitty, swooping on us from the oven, cried, 'Make yourself at home, sir; there's more where these came from. Make a long arm, Miss Patty, and hand them cakes.'

"So we had to devote ourselves to the duties of the table; and Patty, holding the lid with one hand and pouring with the other, supplied Father Christmas's wants with a heavy heart.

"At last he was satisfied. I said grace, during which he stood, and indeed he stood for some time afterwards with his eyes shut—I fancy under the impression that I was still speaking. He had just said a fervent 'Amen,' and reseated himself, when my father put his head into the kitchen, and made this remarkable statement,—

"'Old Father Christmas has sent a tree to the young people.'

"Patty and I uttered a cry of delight, and we forthwith danced round the old man, saying, 'Oh, how nice! Oh, how kind of you!' which I think must have bewildered him, but he only smiled and nodded.

"'Come along," said my father. 'Come children. Come Reuben. Come Kitty.'

"And he went into the parlour, and we all followed him.

"My godmother's picture of a Christmas-tree was very pretty; and the flames of the candles were so naturally done in red and yellow, that I always wondered that they did not shine at night. But the picture was nothing to the reality. We had been sitting almost in the dark, for, as Kitty said, 'Firelight was quite enough to burn at meal-times.' And when the parlour door was thrown open, and the tree, with lighted tapers on all the branches, burst upon our view, the blaze was dazzling, and threw such a glory round the little gifts, and the bags of coloured muslin with acid drops, and pink rose drops, and comfits inside, as I shall never forget. We all got something; and Patty and I, at any rate, believed that the things came from the stores of Old Father Christmas. We were not undeceived even by his gratefully accepting a bundle of old clothes which had been hastily put together to form his present.

"We were all very happy; even Kitty, I think, though she kept her sleeves rolled up, and seemed rather to grudge enjoying herself (a weak point in some energetic characters). She went back to her oven before the lights were out, and the angel on the top of the tree taken down. She locked up her present (a little work-box) at once. She often showed it off afterwards, but it was kept in the same bit of tissue paper till she died. Our presents certainly did not last so long!

"The old man died about a week afterwards, so we never made his acquaintance as a common personage.